essentials
Springer essentials

Springer essentials provide up-to-date knowledge in a concentrated form. They aim to deliver the essence of what counts as "state-of-the-art" in the current academic discussion or in practice. With their quick, uncomplicated and comprehensible information, essentials provide:

- an introduction to a current issue within your field of expertise
- an introduction to a new topic of interest
- an insight, in order to be able to join in the discussion on a particular topic

Available in electronic and printed format, the books present expert knowledge from Springer specialist authors in a compact form. They are particularly suitable for use as eBooks on tablet PCs, eBook readers and smartphones. *Springer essentials* form modules of knowledge from the areas economics, social sciences and humanities, technology and natural sciences, as well as from medicine, psychology and health professions, written by renowned Springer-authors across many disciplines.

Maren Metz · Birgit Spies

Digital Psychology

Classification, Fields of Work and Research

 Springer

Maren Metz
Fachbereich Gesundheit und Pflege
HFH · Hamburger Fern-Hochschule
Hamburg, Germany

Birgit Spies
Fachbereich onlineplus
Hochschule Fresenius
Köln, Germany

ISSN 2731-3107   ISSN 2731-3115   (electronic)
essentials
ISBN 978-3-658-40338-6   ISBN 978-3-658-40339-3   (eBook)
https://doi.org/10.1007/978-3-658-40339-3

Lektorat : Brechtel-Wahl Eva

This Springer imprint is published by the registered company Springer Fachmedien Wiesbaden
GmbH, part of Springer Nature.
The registered company address is: Abraham-Lincoln-Str. 46, 65189 Wiesbaden, Germany

What You Can Find in This *Essential*:

- The book brings together information and current knowledge on psychology and digitalization and condenses it into an overview and outlook.
- Definitions are proposed, boundaries are drawn, and the evolving field of digital psychology is described.
- Furthermore, possibilities and limits are pointed out, and fields of development and research, especially for psychologists, are outlined.
- The book encourages psychologists to actively shape the highly topical field of digital psychology.
- It also offers a variety of starting points and encourages discussion, further development, and further publication.

Contents

About the Authors

Maren Metz The author studied psychology and business psychology at the University of Bremen and earned her doctorate in online coaching at Helmut Schmidt University/University of the Federal Armed Forces Hamburg. She has experience in science and research in the fields of (virtual) learning and change strategies and especially in e-coaching. She is co-editor and author of the books *E-Coaching and Online-Advice: Formats, Concepts, Discussions* and *Digital Learning World – Serious Games: Use in Professional Development*. Not only theoretically but also as a practitioner, she introduces modern media into higher education. She also accompanies change processes in business and is active as a coach and trainer. She is head of the Psychology course at the Department of Health and Care at the HFH – Hamburger Fern-Hochschule.

Birgit Spies The author studied information technology in Dresden and media and education in Rostock with a focus on media psychology and media philosophy. She completed her doctorate at Ludwig-Maximilians-Universität in Munich on the topic "Informal Learning in Social Online Networks." Her professional career has taken her to large German companies as a project manager, trainer, and e-learning developer. As an e-learning expert, she advises companies on digital education and coaches trainers and lecturers for the virtual space. For more than 25 years, she has also taught and lectured on media education topics in adult education and training. At the Fresenius University of Applied Sciences, she holds the professorship for education and digitalization and heads the distance learning program Media and Communication Management (B.A.). Her work and research interests focus in particular on teaching and learning with digital media and education.

Introduction

1

The term "digital" has long ceased to refer to the technically digital in its original understanding. Since the 2010s, "1" and "0" used to encode the transmission of information has become a synonym that encompasses the application of digital technologies in the private, economic, political and social spheres. According to Sühlmann-Faul (2019), digitalization is a transformation that is comprehensive and society-wide and means much more than the use of computers or the networking of people. Digitalization changes, for example, our *communication* and thus the *relationships* – the relating to each other – of people. It is creating **social relationship networks** that enable *connectedness* and *exchange* over great distances. It is changing the *way* work processes are carried out in companies, hospitals and banks, for example. It is also changing the way education and leisure time are organized, as well as the development of *identities* and *communities*. The digital transformation poses fundamental challenges for companies, but also for society as a whole (Boes et al. 2018, p. 76). And the less the mass media can maintain its gatekeeper function - the pre-filtering of information - the more digitalization also influences how we see the world. The so-called media digital power of the networked many has its own dynamics to describe, share and comment on events in the world[1].

Digital innovations can be found, for example, in biotechnology and nanotechnology, in robotics, in artificial intelligence and in the applications of virtual and augmented reality. The buzzwords 'Big Data' and 'Internet of Things' denote changes whose effects we can hardly anticipate at present and whose potential for change can hardly be estimated. According to the German Advisory Council on

---

[1] YouTube Video https://netzpolitik.org/2015/bernhard-poerksen-auf-der-rp15-die-fuenfte-gewalt-die-macht-der-vernetzten-vielen/

M. Metz, B. Spies, *Digital Psychology*, essentials,
https://doi.org/10.1007/978-3-658-40339-3_1

Global Change (WBGU) (2011), these social and individual changes are the mega-trends of our time.

To participate in society, as well as to deal with the changes in the world of work initiated by digitalization, *key digital skills* (competences to work and live in a digitalized environment), *technological skills* (specialist knowledge) and further *qualifications* (skills such as adaptability, creativity or stamina) are needed. According to Stifterverband (2020), these three categories belong to the so-called "future skills" (p. 3). On the other hand, previously required competencies, skills and abilities will become less important. Patience, attention and retentiveness, for example, seem to deteriorate in the face of digital change. Acquiring digital media skills, developing an understanding (in the sense of comprehension) of the dynamics of digitalization, using digital tools in one's own work – all these contribute to psychologists' better understanding of the changes themselves as well as to finding their way with the changes. It is important to **shape** this **social upheaval** also as psychological experts.

Digitalization challenges the human way of thinking even more, especially research on artificial life and artificial intelligence (Rohde 2013). With a digital living and working space, a **digital culture is** emerging in this very space, which is both shaped by people and shapes people themselves. Therefore, it can be assumed that psychological paradigms take hold and, in turn, can shape changes themselves. Typical facets of a culture, such as convictions, moral-ethical understanding, attitudes, customs, practices, language and rituals, change or emerge completely new. At the same time, the focus is shifting to the transformation of society with a view to sustainable developments, in which the possibilities of future generations must be taken into account. This also presupposes an emancipatory and society-changing potential (Görgen and Wendt 2015). All cultural activities are always accompanied by affects and are assigned a value. In particular, the interplay between feelings and reason influences digital development (Damasio 2017, p. 13). According to WBGU (2018), the current conception of mankind will change and thus entail a change in culture. The development of digitalization with its overwhelming influence on humans requires a guiding orientation "that places people – and not technology – at the centre of change" (Boes et al. 2018, p. 78). Social and political shaping of digital transformation is needed (Boes et al. 2018). However, the landscape of digital transformation is much wider. One example is the development of a *collective world consciousness* (WBGU 2019a, b). This is particularly about motivated, sustainable and environmentally conscious human action and the emergence of a corresponding awareness of problems. Digital technologies continue to change our communication structures and create new *forms of participation* and *knowledge appropriation*. Here, too, a public discourse is desirable. There is a need for new guiding principles for a digital, sustainable world of work, but also for these worlds of work to be embedded in society and for people to reflect on their role in them (WBGU 2019a, b). Therefore, the WBGU calls for actively shaping digitalization, analysing and understanding it, exchanging views on it and networking through global partnerships. Humans – and here psychologists in particular - are called upon and will (have to) position themselves in this digitalization process.

Psychology and the Digital World

The roots of psychology reach far back into history. The discipline in its self-understanding was and is always subject to many changes. Now psychology seems to be called upon once again to put all its findings and knowledge at the service of society. Mergers of companies, reorganization and compression of work seem to be part of everyday life. Even private life is not unaffected by digitalization. In addition to many conveniences, we are confronted, among other things, with the fear of our own insignificance and the loss of creative freedom. This inhibits the inherent potential of people to perceive, accept and shape change.

2.1 Psychology as a Developing Branch of Science

Inherent in the historical development and establishment of psychology is the need to constantly evolve and merge with other disciplines. This is achieved with varying speed and success. With the topic of digitalization, fears about the significance of previous fields of activity are also added. The vdek Future Forum 2019, for example, summed up this uncertainty with the title "Is digitalization doing away with psychotherapists?" (vdek 2019). Dependencies on technical devices and digital (social) platforms are growing. The effects will become apparent in a few years. The human being, the "Me", becomes a *public Me in the digital space*. On the one hand, this leads to new possibilities of identity formation, but on the other hand, confronts the "Me" with extreme feedback processes. In no way are judgmental, dysfunctional or media-critical aspects to be the focus here. But they should be named in order to underline the urgency of action. The possibilities, opportunities and also limitations of digitalization in the private environment, the field of work and science of psychology and therapy must be named and discussed. Recommendations for action can then be derived on a reliable basis. The scientific field of psychology is closely linked to changes in society and pursues the goal of describing, explaining and predicting human experience and behaviour. Among other things, work processes change when technology and digitalization processes take hold; the way of life of the individual and the community changes when communication and exchange are strongly digitally organized; and previously unthought-of phenomena, such as the dissolution of the private sphere and the questioning of the credibility of authorities, of media, even of truth itself, are added. The image of humanity is changing: the view of ourselves and of others, which seems to be increasingly shaped by digital self-representation and self-referencing, is in flux.

Psychologists should once again deal with the question of how they can assume *social responsibility* with their work. Explaining and forecasting phenomena no longer seems sufficient. On the one hand, (digital) psychology must act in the sense of critical enlightenment, raise its voice and take a stand. On the other hand, it must promote and demand developments. For example, analogous to the health risk assessment that is advised in companies, an assessment of the risk posed by digitalization can be demanded and developed. Recommendations are no longer sufficient. The findings of (digital) psychology demand to be heard and taken into account, in the sense of *salutogenesis* (Damasio 2017) – so that people can live in a psychologically healthy way in a digitalized world, and so that people are given a *meaning*.

For a long time, scientists have also been pointing out the psychological consequences of the economisation of almost all areas of life (cf. Verhaeghe 2013). Here, the consequences of reduced autonomy of the individual in work and society and increasing pressure to conform (cf. Pauen and Welzer 2015) can be mentioned as well as the change in thinking, behaviour and feeling as a result of hyperconnectedness (cf. Christakis and Fowler 2011). Likewise, the change in "relations of recognition in families, the world of work and the political public sphere" (Honneth 2015, p. 81) must be named, which deprives people of their "customary esteem" (ibid.). Digital technologies *shape* us as social beings and "*shape* our self-image from the inside out" (Floridi 2015, p. 73). As such, they touch our innermost being and must become the focus of psychological research.

What do all these changes do to us? There are many questions that need to be clarified. Well-known psychological models and theories need to be examined for their applicability to our digitally shaped lives, and new theoretical models need to be developed. In particular, it is important not only to approach fields outside the discipline, but also to consciously look for ways in which psychological expertise can be linked to the findings and research of other disciplines. In some cases, technical and digital possibilities from fields outside the discipline are already being used for the purposes of psychology and psychotherapy. For example, various technological wearables and gadgets can be used to record moods and biological data, which can then be used in psychoeducation. Applications from telemedicine can offer low-threshold access to therapeutic help. Developments in artificial intelligence can help to overcome fears and phobias.

The further development of psychology also includes a *further development* and, if necessary, a *reorientation of* psychologists. This begins with digitalization and the internet-based provision of specialist knowledge, and the creation of platforms and forums where people can obtain sound psychological knowledge. It continues with a conscious networking of experts among themselves, including digital possibilities such as web meetings and virtual congresses. The developing digital competence of psychologists must also include the natural application of e-coaching and e-counselling.

2.2 Origin and Current Development

A science such as psychology, which in its self-image is constantly changing, is called upon to play an active role in shaping processes of change. Interdisciplinary cooperation in the development of technical and digital innovations is just as necessary as anticipating their consequences.

Standing on the sidelines and *subsequently researching* the effects of already established technologies can **only uncover,** but **not shape.** Digitization and research, such as that on artificial intelligence, pose the old question about the relationship between mankind and technology anew: What is mankind? When the symbiotic relationship between mankind and (digital) machine seems to deepen further: Where does the human or being human begin, where does he/she end? What influence does this have on our thinking, feeling and behaviour?

Understanding digitization means accessing the digital world and thereby making it more objectified. In particular, this means creating spaces in this world, using and shaping them (Deinet et al. 2018). Through synthesis performance, people succeed in linking different life-world references with the digital (Löw 2001). The *(self)motivation* causes an engagement with the digital environment in order to exist in it and *creatively* create *spaces of encounter and identity.* This can be an individual or collective process of appropriation and design.

2.2.1   Development of Psychology with Regard to Digitalization

While psychology was initially concerned with immediate human experience and behaviour in its origins, since the inventions of the industrial age of the late eighteenth century, the mainframe computer in the 1940s, the entry of the television into homes in the 1950s, and the computer in the 1980s-to name just a few salient points-it has been clear that technology and media (and today expanded to include the digital) interact with humans and their psyches. People create things, techniques and rituals. The way they use them has an effect on what they create. Both sides influence and change each other.

Now, technical, media and digital development – as well as cultural development – can have various causal reasons, such as the *physical* and *cognitive relief of* humans themselves (e.g. lifting tools, robots and computers), for companies faster work processes and increasing profits (e.g. assembly line production and commodity databases) and for the efficient administration and communication of the State (e.g. digitalization of civil registers and electronic application processing, such as the submission of tax returns). Although technical and digital developments were intended to support and possibly even replace human performance, there was also a growing awareness of their limitations. On the one hand, technical developments helped to make the understanding of human processes tangible and technically representable. Cognitive psychology, for example, combined biological findings with psychological processes and translated them into technical functions. On the other hand, in the 1980s the idea that human experience and behaviour can be much more multifaceted, and that it is difficult to fit it into a programmable schedule became more and more important.

Media psychology, as a sub-field of psychology, began to establish itself and turned to questions that had previously remained rather unnoticed. The cognitive and emotional processing of media content, the use of media and digital offerings for learning and knowledge processes, technology- and computer-mediated communication, the analysis of human-machine/computer interaction and the experience of virtual reality – these and other questions were now increasingly researched, and an interdisciplinary view was once again required. With digitization, a complex phenomenon has now moved into the social focus, which has a lasting impact on all areas of life, work and society – in the sense of having a long-lasting effect and changing things – whether we like it or not. Previous fields of work and expertise no longer seem sufficient to describe the phenomena of digitization, to research them and, based on this, to offer forecasts and recommendations for people and society.

Two variants seem possible: (1) disciplines *expand* their own field **of work** and **research** to include issues of digitalization and thereby look at psychological issues, or (2) a **separate discipline** emerges: **digital psychology**. This looks at the digitalization of different areas of life from a psychological perspective and can and should seek to find its way into other disciplines.

Following the core questions of media psychology (Batinic and Appel 2008), digital psychology can be outlined in terms of content as follows:

1.   What does digitalization do to people?

This question is related to the effects and consequences of digitalization.

2.   What do people do with digitalization?

The focus here is on the use of digital technologies.

In order to develop into a discipline of its own – digital psychology – such a discipline should incorporate theories and concepts from other *psychological subfields,* such as general psychology, social, developmental and media psychology, as well as concepts, models and theory from the *fields* of computer science and engineering, systems theory and cybernetics, communication and media studies, philosophy and cultural studies, among others. It is also advisable to include influences from constructivism, cybernetics, systems theory and Gestalt psychology, because this is where technology, computer science and psychology meet. Psychology, in contrast to computer science, is concerned with individual rather than automated information processing.

Figure 2.1 below shows a sketchy overview of the professional influences on digital psychology, which will continue to evolve.

2.2.2   Location of Digital Psychology

Here, an attempt is first made to classify digital psychology in the existing research landscape. Furthermore, fields of work are identified, and research questions are assigned in order to give digital psychology an initial structuring and systematization.

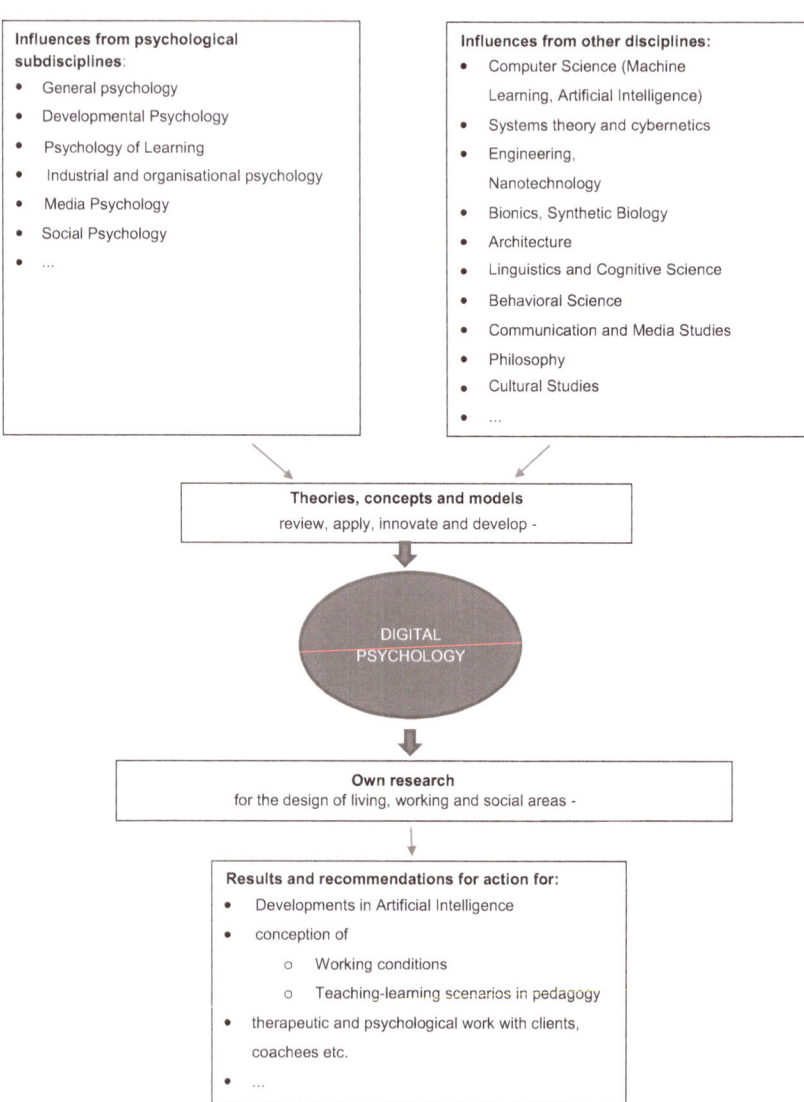

Fig. 2.1 Influences and theories from psychological subfields and other disciplines on digital psychology

Where can the new discipline be rooted in psychological science? Digital psychology can be classified as a **special field of** psychology. It is committed to concept and theory development, the elaboration and testing of research paradigms and specific methods, but also to the assumption of evaluation and design science tasks. The special field of digital psychology leans on **applied sub-disciplines.** Digital psychology incorporates findings from general psychology (e.g. on perception, attention and emotions), personality psychology (e.g. on inter- and intra-individual differences in dealing with digital media and digitalization) and social psychology (e.g. on collective reactions such as public outcries).

Cognitive psychology also contributes important findings on information processing (cognition), such as findings on perception or knowledge acquisition. Digital psychology is thus enriched by *basic disciplines* but located in *application disciplines.* Digital psychology is developing in the direction of a **practical psychology** that emerges as a by-product of technological innovations. This psychological discipline requires a theoretical foundation (theoretical psychology). The insights gained in this way in turn flow into the paradigms of applied psychology, which not only analyses and evaluates, but also proposes and implements solutions.

Following Trepte and Reinecke (2013, p. 15f.), the following definition is proposed for digital psychology and digitization, which at the same time highlights the necessity of this special discipline.

Digital psychology deals with the description, explanation and prediction of experience and behaviour in connection with digitalization.

Digitalization means the use of digital technologies in all areas of life, work and society, which results in the change of processes, events and structures and thus has an impact on human experience and behaviour.

Digital psychology describes **mental processes in the digital space,** as well as the complex psychological mechanisms of **human feeling, thinking** and **behaviour** that arise as a result of digitalization. This includes internal and external causes and conditions, such as individual and collective *experience* and *consciousness*, and the resulting experiential values. Figure 2.2 below outlines the location of digital psychology.

Taking up the core questions of digital psychology formulated above, the view and the research interest of such a special discipline must clearly be broadened. Digitization must be recognised as a trigger for a wide range of changes, the effects

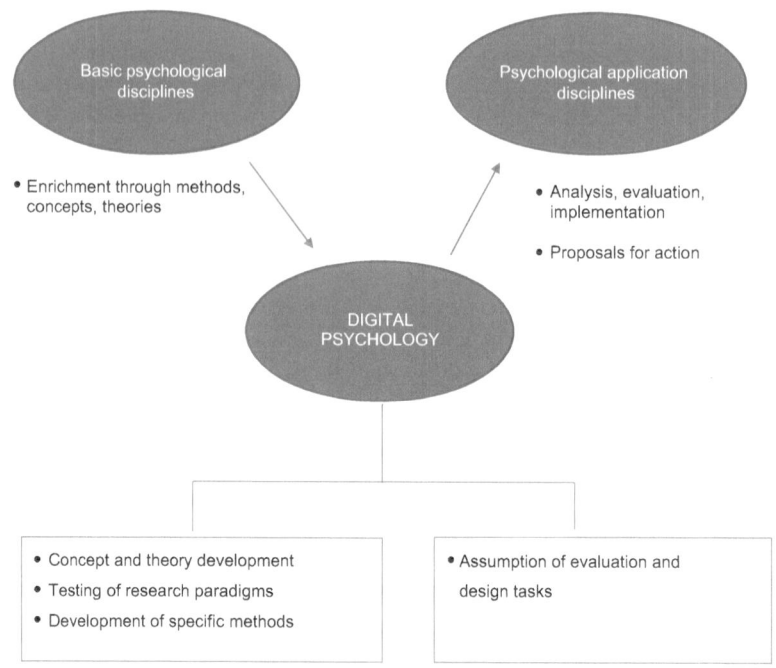

Fig. 2.2 Location of digital psychology

and scope of which have not been foreseeable to date. Through digital technologies, processes in everyday life and work are seemingly optimized, including one's own life. Entirely new business models are emerging, as a result of which entire industries are collapsing and disappearing from the world of work. The acquisition of knowledge is changing the educational landscape, covering it with evaluations and learning analytics, also striving for efficiency and optimization. The perception and evaluation of events is linked to digital presence, among other things. Individuals and actors from business, science and politics influence each other in their actions. In the process, structures and system relationships are steadily becoming more complex and more opaque, leading to "lifeworld consequences and psychological stress" (Ziemann 2011, p. 14).

Digital space has long since become a *real space,* even if it is not materially tangible. People act in digital space and use digital technologies more or less as a matter of course. A separation of the two spaces can no longer be maintained. And yet: "Ultimately, experience and behaviour is always an interaction between situation and person" (Kuhl et al. 2010, p. 21). For the field of digital psychology, it will be interesting to find out what goals and intentions people pursue in the context of digitalization, what actions they are prompted or encouraged to take by the very same. It will be necessary to research what behaviour people display, what behavioural routines they develop, and what affects will be associated with digitization.

2.2.3   Fields of Work and Research

Following the definition of psychology, it is advisable, in addition to fields of work and research, to consider concrete questions and hypotheses of a digital psychology from three perspectives: (1) emotion, (2) cognition, (3) behaviour. These perspectives can also be assigned to different levels: (a) individual level, (b) community (social and cultural) level, (c) economic and work-related level, (d) societal and political level. In the following, initial questions are formulated and classified.

(1) **Individual level**
   Emotion perspective:

- How do people feel about the high dynamics of the development of digitalization?
- Is digitalization judged to be beneficial to life?
- How does the experience of self-efficacy change through digitalization and the use of digital applications?
- How do emotions find expression in digital space?
- What mental experiences are evoked by the inner images and feelings triggered in the digital space?
- Which aspects of the digital world influence the experience of the inner world – the feelings and the weighting of these – in terms of homeostasis?

Cognition perspective:

- How does digital information acquisition change thinking (perceiving, storing, remembering)?
- Do digitization and digital space allow sufficient opportunity for thought association and the processing of cognitive processes?
- Is the experience in the digital space characterized more by activity or passivity?
- How do self-regulation and stress management take place in the digital space?

- Is ego control changing in the digital space as well as through digital processes?
- Are self-control and discipline different in the digital space?
- Can digital applications support self-efficacy?

- What impact do digital applications have on individual competences?

Behavioural perspective:

- How do people use digital technologies?
- How do relationships and the way people interact with each other change in the digital space?

(2) **Community level (social and cultural)**
Emotion perspective:

- To what extent does digital space create a sense of being or subjectivity? Can a process of subjectivity emerge?
- Is the person in the digital space in a consciousness-reflecting process? Is he aware of the accompanying inner images and feelings?

Cognition perspective:

- Is the digital space a social meeting place for exchange and social interaction?
- To what extent do attention, cognition, and emotion change in a digital group?
- Does altruistic behaviour take place in the digital space? Is this enhanced or diminished by digitalization?
- How does communication change?
- How are inner images of mentalizing digital space ordered into a narrative?
- What social behaviours have emerged through digitization and the digital space?
- How do impact-oriented motives such as achievement and power show up?
- Do personality traits influence behaviour in the digital space?
- Do an individual's attitudes and values influence how they deal with digitalization and how they behave in the digital space?
- Does digitalization create new spaces for creativity? What impact does this have on society, culture, work and the individual?

Behavioural perspective:

- Does cooperative action emerge in the digital space? What cooperative behaviours are evident here?
- Does digitalization and the use of digital technologies change the way people behave towards each other?
- Does the outside world influence the design of digital space?
- How does society change when human intelligence is emulated by technical systems?
- How do communication of and relationships in communities change in the digital space?

(3) **Economic and labour level**
Behavioural perspective:

- How are digital offerings being used in the context of psychotherapy, and are they changing as a result?
- Are there positive supply effects through digital structures, offers and methods?
- Is there a need for psychological and therapeutic digital applications (such as apps)?
- What standards must be met for the integration of digital methods in psychotherapy?
- What impact does digitalization have on psychotherapeutic work and psychotherapeutic care?
- How do psychotherapists acquire digital competence?
- How can the development of artificial intelligence be shaped?

(4) **Social and political level**
Behavioural perspective:

- How can individual transparency, privacy and self-determination be preserved in the face of big data?
- Does digitalization attack human dignity? How can this be protected?

The first approaches to machine learning were inspired by psychological research, and so it seems helpful to classify digital psychology under this focus. If we look at current research on artificial intelligence, we see that it is also composed of many highly specialized subfields of cognitive science: language and image understanding and production, planning, knowledge representation, learning, problem solving, and reasoning. Since there is often no general efficient solution path in these subdomains, *heuristic methods* are mostly used (Schmidt 2013, p. 45). Through the development of cognitive models, psychological theories have thus also been further developed (Schmidt 2013, p. 46). As an example, theories on the reliability of estimating one's own conclusions can be mentioned here. The ability to metacognize has thus become a very relevant cognitive science research topic. Research on artificial intelligence is assigned to the discipline of experiential science, and psychology thus also fits in well (Schmidt 2013, p. 44).

2.2.4 Development and Application of Digital Technologies in Psychology

Concrete examples of digitization can already be found in psychology. Selected applications are described below.

(1) *Apps, smartphones and tech bracelets.*

Scientists at Harvard University in Cambridge, together with the Massachusetts Institute of Technology (MIT), have developed apps and wristbands that predict people's moods (mood predication). These mood barometers are intended as a kind of early warning system to help people themselves and also to inform others when, for example, a depressive phase is imminent.

Numerous apps can now be used to record and evaluate biological and psychological data. The app Moodpath, for example, is a mood diary developed by psychologists, doctors and scientists. Here, several question times a day are recorded and evaluated over a period of two weeks in total. The user can thus be given indications of depressive symptoms and offered professional help.

(2) *Telemedicine and eHealth*

Doctors and therapists offer digitized methods of consultation and treatment on the basis of the Digital Care Act (Bundesministerium für Gesundheit, 2020). The Versorgungsforschung (Health Services Research) report already presented a wide range of applications from a medical perspective in 2012 (Bartmann and Blettner 2012) and can be inspiring for Digital Psychology. For example, technologies such as nursing glasses make life easier for caregivers by means of augmented reality.

(3) *Psychotherapeutic interventions*

Science and industry are intensively engaged in the application of digital psychotherapeutic interventions. For example, digital applications are being developed that can be used for mental disorders. Based on a gaming design, for example, good results are achieved with spider phobias by means of confrontation therapy and augmented reality (Frauenhofer Institut 2018). The Techniker Krankenkasse (Technicians' Health Insurance) also offers virtual reality therapy for anxiety disorders (TKK 2020).

(4) *E-recruitment*

With the help of artificial intelligence (AI), intelligent action programs are being developed that can take over human activities. In recruitment, for example, AI-based options are used for networking with candidates, for talent search and for so-called candidate experience optimization. This includes all perceptions and experiences that a candidate gathers during the contact and application phase with a company. In aptitude diagnostics, technology-based assessments using artificial intelligence promise valid forecasts of professional performance and the generalizability of the findings.

(5) *Robots and algorithms*

Some research is analyzing people's voices to draw conclusions about their emotions. For example, the Cogito system analyzes the voice of service employees and prompts them to adopt a friendlier tone when they detect unfriendliness.

(6) *Brain-Computer Interfaces*

In recent years, the research field of *brain-computer interfaces (BCI)* has been established as a result of interdisciplinary work between psychologists, medical doctors, computer scientists, neuroscientists, and cognitive scientists (Birbaumer and Matuz 2013; Bundesministerium für Wirtschaft und Energie, 2019). Current research focuses on developing new learning paradigms for maintaining communication skills using BCI systems. As communication has been identified as an essential aspect of quality of life, along with family and other social contacts, alternative means of communication are being made available to ill people through BCI systems. BCI systems can be used to remotely control robots or virtual realities via wireless transmission (Birbaumer and Matuz 2013).

Researchers are also striving to identify the conditions for *minimal consciousness* and to implement them in the structures of artificial systems. Such systems would then have their own consciousness and might even be capable of suffering.

Especially in the field of artificial intelligence, psychologists should contribute their fundamental paradigms and research findings at an early stage. This is the only way to help shape the field of digital psychology and to shape it in the sense of a humanistic image of mankind. However, this does not happen naturally, but requires different (legal, scientific, ethical, financial) frameworks and possibilities in order to meet the typical hurdles of change – taking ethical aspects into account.

2.2.5   On the Naming of the Research Area

It will become clear whether the term *digital psychology* is appropriate for the field of work and research described above. A linguistic approach and a discourse on this are desirable. The terms **cyber psychology, online psychology, virtual**

psychology, e-psychology, psychonics, medial psychology or **technology-based psychology** or something else entirely would also be conceivable.

In the English-speaking world, the term *Cyber Psychology* seems to be establishing itself. The focus of research in *cyber psychology*, a subfield of media psychology, is a phenomenon related to the Internet. This does not seem to be sufficient, as digitalization encompasses much more than just the Internet, even if the latter plays a central role in it. Moreover, the term *cyber psychology* is not unambiguous in the German-speaking world and triggers different associations.

Originating from ancient Greek, *cyber* simply means *control*. With the emergence of the discipline *cybernetics* (in German also cybernetics, the control and regulation technology) in the 1950s, *cyber* also found its way into German usage and is used today, for example, in the security of information and communication technology ("cyber security"). According to Duden (2020), *cyber* refers to a "virtual illusory world created by computers" (Duden 2020). Conceptual limits become apparent here: Even if some phenomena of digitalization are not visible – in the sense of being materially present – like the Internet itself, they do exist and have an impact on our lifeworld. The artificially created world becomes a real world. By using the term *digital psychology*, the emergence of digitization is linguistically acknowledged. The changes brought about by it are thus no longer understood as artificial – as existing only in parts.

This is not just about the name of a development and research area, but also about a process of adaptation and use by people and society. It is likely that digitalization will also change the image of mankind. Will we speak of **Homo Digitalis** in the future? Or does this classification go too far? The argument in favour of such a title is that people only really understand things when they are *discussed*, i.e., when things are given names. Only then does something diffuse become something concrete that people can talk about, think about and reflect upon. But the named also gets a shell, a boundary, which in turn helps people to look at it, to explore it and thus to understand it.

State of Development and Research

So, what might an initial thought framework of digital psychology look like? Systemic adaptations, the complexity of digital spaces, research on artificial intelligence, logic, thinking and human-machine interactions – these are some topics worth looking at.

In the following, some initial ideas are presented in order to inspire further thinking and research.

3.1 Systemic Adaptations

If the **interactions** between **humans and the digital system are** considered, both internal and external limitations of the system can be identified, which virtually challenge adaptation processes. Possibly, observation positions are initially taken that generate *as-if assumptions*. Theoretical assumptions are made that need to be empirically tested. This is not only necessary scientifically, but also along their resonance in the digital space with humans. From this, a possible approach emerges: First, *distinctions* should be analyzed. These can then be worked with, in the sense of description and interpretation, and cognition can develop. The resulting resonance will determine whether the insight proves itself.

What should be described is the emerging *diversity,* the associated *use* and *relationship formation,* but also the *boundaries* and those things that *disappear* through selective processes (Treml 2004). Here it seems helpful to describe the mixture of *chance* and *necessity* that leads to the developmental possibilities rather than the consciously planned developments. It is likely that conscious thinking and planning with conceptual development directed into the future, as well as conscious

M. Metz, B. Spies, *Digital Psychology*, essentials, https://doi.org/10.1007/978-3-658-40339-3_3

reason capable of planning, are not drivers of development (ibid.). The key feature of development is the *process of adaptation.* Adaptations should thus be the focus (ibid.). Two important development factors are *space* and *time.*

The system can adapt in three ways (Treml 2004, p. 84):

1. **The system adapts to its environment.**

Through momentum and adaptation, the system is adjusted so that it can continue to live in its change.

2. **The system adapts the environment to itself.**

The environment is changed so that the system can continue to live in its own changed environment.

3. **The system makes itself independent** of the changing environmental conditions.

It determines its own dependence and independence internally.

How will the digital space change in this respect? What are the adaptations that digitalization demands of people?

Within the *adaptation performance,* which can happen via learning processes, both **correspondence** and **coherence** should be investigated. Correspondence describes the external experience between human and digital space. Coherence structures the internal experience and leads to reorganization (Treml 2004, p. 164). It should be investigated how an adaptation of humans to digitalization and digital space happens, how humans behave under changing conditions, and which opportunities for change they accept. From this, general adaptive capacities of humans in this system could be elaborated. The expectation is not only to explain behaviour, but also to change a previous state. This can be described, for example, by the concept of *education.* Education changes people and creates an active support in the process of change.

Following on from this, there is the question of *learning performance,* which can be observed through changes in behaviour. These observations help to infer the knowledge inherent in the system. The patterns of this learning system should be worked out. For this purpose, the "asymmetry between individual and social motives" (Treml 2004, p. 167) can be considered in more detail, because these decisively shape learning processes. In addition, in *pre-adaptation processes,* the so-called *pre-adaptations,* are to be examined. If one would like to apply *playful exploration* to the field of digitalization, characteristics such as attachment behaviour/relationship behaviour, protective behaviour, sensitivity to social stimuli, such as social attention, should be examined. The necessity of education in connection with digitalization as self- and world-empowerment of mankind (according to Baacke 1996) is evident as such.

3.2 Complexity in the Digital Space

Digital space is a highly complex system in which each person perceives this system selectively depending on their "sensory structure" (Treml 2004, p. 58) and "possible environmental sensitivity" (ibid.). In order to approach this complexity, two criteria are required: an "openness to the diversity of empirical experience on the one hand and [an] order of thinking that is as simple as possible by reducing it to a few distinctions and basic operations on the other" (Treml 2004, p. 11).

The first point of *openness* does not come naturally but is determined by personality and experience. There are people who are averse to digitalization and thus closed off. Only when events are important or useful for the individual do they stimulate thinking and then change. High complexity involves a high degree of *internal differentiation*, which leads to many states. These states of order must be sorted and their patterns worked out. Above all, attention should be paid to repetition, hierarchization, interaction (interdependence) and tradability (Treml 2004).

Humans in the digital space move in a high complexity and with specific adaptation processes, such as **self-organization**. Thus, self-organization is the *adaptive power*. There are the **innovators** who help shape the digital transformation, the **doers** who integrate the ideas into everyday life and make them routine, the **coordinators** who mediate in the complexity of the digital space and the **mentors** who guide through the digital space (Treml 2004). Processes of mentalization are important on the path to active design: 'All mental faculties intervene in the process of human culture' (Damasio 2017, p. 189) and 'feelings are a core – perhaps the core – of mental states' (Damasio 2017, p. 181). Feelings are represented as perceptual maps or images. Digital culture and feelings mutually influence and shape each other, from which a new valence emerges (see Damasio 2017, p. 144). People have the ability to express these inner representations in words and communicate them to others, even if they have not seen them themselves but have sensed or felt them (Damasio 2017, p. 168). In this way, they influence the digital space and developments in it.

In the digital space, people have to collect, store and process a lot of *general* and *permanent* information on the one hand, and as little *specific* and *temporary* information as possible on the other (Treml 2004, p. 98). How well does this work?

Approaching this complex area of the use of digital space requires well-founded theories that must satisfy paradigmatic demands, as well as methodical and controlled expansion.

3.3 Research on Artificial Intelligence

Artificial intelligence (AI) deals with the synthesis of *adaptive life processes* (Rohde 2013). Already in the 1990s, the topic of artificial life became an independent subject area in artificial intelligence research. "Core topics were evolution, adaptation, self-organization, and closed-loop behavior" (Rohde 2013, p. 180). The closed control loop is always spoken of when there is a system that immediately registers the effects of its behaviour in the environment and can react to them in real time (Rohde 2013, p. 180).

The logical-rational can be well represented by algorithms, which a computer needs for decision-making processes. But what a living being needs for its own survival are processes that cannot be understood as pure data processing in the brain, such as the behaviour of nonlinear processes (e.g. in chemical systems) or in self-organization processes such as swarm behavior. Self-organization is understood here as "spontaneous formation of ordered structures through coupling of local processes" (Rohde 2013, p. 182). On the one hand, a natural system should be understood scientifically through exact replication. Thus, a scientific understanding of life, including its cognitive abilities, can be obtained through the replication of adaptive techniques. On the other hand, technical problem solutions should be inspired by nature, or scientific problems should be solved by replicating living organism structures. Here, insights from cognitive science can be incorporated. The aim of cognitive science is to identify cognitive processes that can be modelled as efficiently as possible by digital processes. In cognitive science, the fundamental question is the "computational solution path of a task" (Huth 2013, p. 42), which also explains information-processing processes in humans. The "understanding of the simple living being is the key to understanding cognition and human intelligence" (Rohde 2013, p. 181). The overall goal is to not only be able to make predictions through simulations, but to develop a simulation for the *cognitive process* itself.

In recent years, there has been a philosophical debate about artificial intelligence and the possibilities of *real thought* and *consciousness of* such **superintelligences.** Artificial intelligence will always evolve through technology, so there is a call for an intellectual awakening, especially from philosophy. Shouldn't psychology also consciously approach this topic and investigate the question whether machines can be capable of empathy and mentalization, perhaps even capable of feelings such as suffering or shame?

The idea that information-processing processes can also be simulated in computers and thus implemented is the basis for *artificial intelligence research*. Artificial intelligence research is a part of computer science that deals with the conception of the formalization, characterization, implementation and evaluation of algorithms. The goal is to use algorithms to solve problems that previously could only be solved with human intelligence (Schmidt 2013). This involves general solutions that are then solved by cognitive systems. In particular, the processes of living organisms are to be emulated.

The overall goal is to grasp and solve problems and to gain a general understanding of animal and human cognitive processes. This involves the *representation, use* and *expansion of* knowledge (Huth 2013). This is accomplished with so-called *artifacts*. These are programs that are executed by a computer or a robot. In particular, topics concerning the "complexity, computability, and selectability of problems or their solution" are investigated (Schmidt 2013, p. 44). Since this perspective on the development of these systems is rather narrow; psychological, biological or neuropsychiatric findings are considered in the extension. Artificial intelligence systems not only claim to solve a problem in an intelligent and efficient way, but to do so in a similar way to a human (Schmidt 2013). Since AI systems are often interactive, "known characteristics and limitations of human information processing should be taken into account" (Schmidt 2013, p. 44). For solving a problem with numerous solution paths, the one that most naturally represents humans is preferred. Therefore, knowledge about human knowledge representation and human problem-solving strategies is important. The connection between psychological knowledge and (new) algorithms is what Schmidt (2013) calls **psychonics.**

The field of symbol-processing artificial intelligence is concerned with *internal representation*. Its challenge is that behaviour in a closed loop cannot always be programmed by an internal replication of the environment. Artificial intelligence research distinguishes *Strong AI, Universal AI, Weak AI* and *Cognitive AI:* **Strong AI** is understood to be programmed artificial intelligence that fully replicates general human intelligence (Huth 2013, p. 43). This means that humans are able to develop an artificial intelligence that is indistinguishable from human intelligence. Such an artificial intelligence does not yet exist (Gabriel 2018).

By a **Universal AI,** Gabriel (2018) understands an artificial intelligence that can switch from one intelligent activity to another at the appropriate moment. Such an artificial intelligence has also not yet been realized. In particular, in the AI application, the so-called *deep learning* comes into focus. This is about the self-learning capabilities of machines and finding independent solutions to previously unsolved problems with the help of optimized algorithms.

Weak AI describes pragmatic intelligent solution strategies that involve supporting expert systems and classification or planning algorithms "that exceed human capabilities in their specific and limited application areas precisely because of their otherness and no longer even claim to be true replicas" (Huth 2013, p. 43).

Cognitive AI aims at the so-called Strong AI, namely the development of algorithms and systems that are similar to human processes of information processing. Cognitive models or cognitive architectures of computer simulations can be mentioned here as examples (Schmidt 2013). "In contrast to standard AI systems, which essentially represent internal "thinking" processes, autonomous agents are characterized by the fact that they *act* in interaction with the environment" (Schmidt 2013, p. 46). In robotics, autonomous agents are endowed with corporeality.

Artificial systems can also be designed to be intelligent or even more intelligent than humans. It is also possible to program moral values and corresponding reactions for artificial systems, but these cannot (yet) be built or modified independently. Artificial systems also cannot (yet) generate their own feelings. Moreover, artificial systems cannot (yet) *mentally* experience values, feelings and related action themselves (Damasio 2017, p. 231). Moreover, no degree of freedom can (yet) be used in thinking and feeling.

These demarcations, the awareness of the differences, especially the different strengths, is an important emancipation process so that the individual can find his role in the changing system and live in it. People use algorithms in their daily lives, but they themselves *are* not algorithms (Damasio 2017, p. 228). Human behaviour and actions are also not subject to algorithms. Thus, humans are not necessarily predictable and cannot be artificially replaced.

As a specialist psychological discipline, digital psychology is particularly called upon to contribute to developments in artificial intelligence. Existing knowledge, for example of media philosophy and media ethics, can be used and expanded with a view to technology assessment of digital developments (What is all this doing to us?). Likewise, the subject area is in demand in the context of discussions about *technology ethics* and *data ethics. It* is not about critical or euphoric views, but about how we can do one without leaving the other.

3.4   Logic, Thinking and Artificial Intelligence

If Gabriel (2018) is correct, then the *digital age* is "an age of the domination of logic over human thought" (Gabriel 2018, p. 145). The foundations of this age are logic and mathematics. "Logic is the study of the determination of relations between thoughts" (Gabriel 2018, p. 143). Logic includes thinking. "Logic is concerned with working out logical laws from the existing material of human thought" (Gabriel 2018, p. 144). Human thought is not very logical and therefore difficult to replicate by algorithms.

People, for example, accept errors in their everyday thinking and actions through their deliberation and through their momentary personal and emotional state in order to act quickly and obtain a result. Thus, the **replication of human thinking** is not so much about how humans think, but how they should think if they wanted to behave rationally and thus also try to avoid erroneous conclusions. The question arises whether *artificial intelligence* can think; that is, whether it can be understood as a process of data processing that is programmable. Gabriel (2018) understands AI as a model of thought, a logical map of human thought. Artificial intelligence is therefore "not a copy of human thought" (Gabriel 2018, p. 146). However, there seems to be a desire to orient human thinking towards logic as a target concept. Thinking arises not only in a linguistic process, but also in an unconscious, non-verbal realm. Therefore, Gabriel sees copying the thinking process as unfeasible at present.

Psychology looks at the actual thinking of human beings. "Logic and psychology are therefore two principally different sciences" (Gabriel 2018, p. 145). Logic in digitization, however, goes beyond human thinking. Artificial intelligence attempts to harness "a pure logic decoupled from human thought" (Gabriel 2018, p. 145) through logical operations that can be mapped mathematically and programmed as software. With this consideration, Gabriel (2018) opposes a possible form of *computational psychology*. Logic is thus the limit of artificial intelligence. It delimits the framework of the thinkable, the boundary of thought that cannot be crossed (ibid.).

Comparison of human and artificial intelligence

Human intelligence	Artificial intelligence
Acts on the basis of thinking	Operates in a logical thought model
Uses intelligence (the ability to think)	Uses logic (the laws of thinking)
Contexts of thought emerge from a complex interaction	Thoughts are based on logical programmed laws
Since people understand things, they also have the capacity to think	The AI itself is not intelligent

(continued)

(continued)

Human intelligence	Artificial intelligence
With consciousness, preconsciousness and subconsciousness	Unconscious
Mental states	No mental states
Capable of semantics (the study of meaning)	
Knowledge of truth due to the interplay of thoughts and reality	
Reality is given meaning. (Projection thesis)	
Strong thinking and reflection skills	
Moral attitude, sentiment and obligation	
Emotional timbre of life	
Practise pattern recognition	Practise pattern recognition
Adapt to a limited section of reality	Adapt to a comprehensive section of reality
Emotional bond	Emotional attachment through programmed value assumptions
	Low error rate in routines
May fall ill	Can be infected by viruses, can break, needs a software update
In the analogue reality	In the digital reality

3.5   Human-Machine Interaction

The WBGU (2019a, b) sees the benefits of digitalization in *humanity coming into its own.* "AI would possibly allow us to emancipate ourselves from it to a certain extent and permit a stronger hint towards abilities such as empathy, caring and solidarity" (WBGU 2019a, b, p. 7). Humans also create companions for themselves, such as digital assistants, which free humans from monotonous activities and support them, for example, in learning and understanding. Humans may also create superintelligence and thus "ensouled artificial entities with autonomous volition and reproduction in a later phase of the digital revolution" (WBGU 2019a, b, p. 7). A *new humanism is* emerging as a culture of cooperation, empathy and global solidarity become central (WBGU 2019a, b). In addition, human beings have to deal with the possibilities of digitalization in their ethical stance. This is also happening in the context of human-machine collaboration*, interaction* and possible future human-machine partnership.

Human-Machine Interaction is an interdisciplinary field that incorporates research from cognitive science, computer science, artificial intelligence research, software ergonomics, design, and the sociology of technology. New findings from *general psychology* (e.g., perception psychology and motivation, emotion and volition research) and *differential and personality psychology* (e.g., the development and modelling of personality and intelligence research) as well as *media psychology* (*e.g., media* effects and *media* selection) are also taken into account. Psychology contributes in particular its knowledge of human *experience* and *behaviour,* their internal and external *causes, conditions* and their *development.* Here, the findings on conscious and unconscious processes and their experience, especially on *cognitive processes,* i.e., the processing of information within human thinking and decision-making, are important. Implications for *user-friendly* design of software and technical systems can be derived from psychological findings, and the interactions between humans and machines can be improved (Wachsmuth 2013).

The systems embodied in *computer science,* so-called cognitive **robotics,** aim to transfer general problems to autonomously acting robots. Psychological insights, especially from the representation and processing of knowledge, are incorporated here. The robot is supposed to combine explicit knowledge of given tasks with action. To do this, the robot must have *categories* of *objects* and *locations.* Other robot architectures, for example those in industrial robotics, can do without this addition. Reactively controlled robots, on the other hand, can dispense with *internal presentations* of explicit knowledge. In cognitive robotics*, situated, embodied, augmented,* and *enacted cognition* are important (Huth 2013, p. 43). So far, a major challenge in cognitive robotics is to fuse sensory data, i.e., to create simultaneous localization and mapping, and then to relate it to itself (ibid.).

Cognitive robotics can be understood as a subfield of robotics, but it is also a line of work of autonomous mobile robots that deals with knowledge representation or its problems in artificial intelligence research (Hertzberg 2013).

The cognitive in the term *cognitive robotics* describes the desired capabilities of the robot:

> to act in a targeted manner under real-time conditions and to do so under uncertain information about their environment and the effect of their own actions, as embedded systems under continuous processing of sensor data from the environment (...), using relevant explicit knowledge (...) and with a high degree of autonomy (Hertzberg 2013, p. 47).

The goal is for the robot not only to perceive its environment in semantic categories, but also to be able to incorporate the **specific manipulation of objects,** which has not yet been achieved (Hertzberg 2013, p. 51).

Communication, cognitive performance and the understanding and production of *speech, gestures* and *facial expressions* in a dialogue fall into the range of transferability of *natural interaction* between humans and machines. Likewise, the possibility of human-technology cooperation in the sense of an artificial interlocutor can be added. Examples can be the **social robot** (in the real physical world) or the *autonomous humanoid-looking robot* in a simulated computer-graphic environment of a virtual world. Virtual reality is gaining importance in this context because it combines sensory and actuator capabilities of humans with the synthetic world of the computer. In addition, there are efforts to build support systems that can take over interactions with the help of intelligent techniques and assistance tasks (Sullivan and Tyler 1991).

The vision is to let technical systems find solutions on *their own*. Such an intelligent technology is called an *interface agent*. An interface agent observes activities in the environment, initiates communication and acts as an autonomous entity, thus performing tasks independently (Wachsmuth 2013). Computer animated figures *with* **synthetic characters,** called *virtual agents,* can also become artificial interlocutors. Thinking further, these agents could possess so-called *mental properties* such as knowledge, motivation, intention, conviction, desire, or commitment, which are modeled on the character traits of a human (Rao and Geotgeff 1991). The aim is to realize a shared knowledge of goals and their solidary pursuit (Wachsmuth 2013), which can create a *shared mental model of reality*. For this, these agents need their own modelled personality with integrated *emotion model, autonomous action* and *communication style*. They would then follow social patterns of interpersonal interaction and act like a social counterpart. With these capabilities, the perceived action, the view of the human on the artificial agent shifts – from the use of an application to a partnership.

Practical Example of Avatar-Based Coaching

In the field of online-based coaching, the first artificial agents as avatars are taking shape. In 1980, the MUD (Multi User Dungeon) project enabled people to experience a shared virtual world for the first time (Bartle 2006). Here, a game was integrated into the MUD collaboration platform.

Today, avatar-based coaching offers immersion in a virtual world with an immersive effect, i.e., a simultaneous *mental immersion in an artificial world*. The term immersion describes the real sensation of a person in a virtual environment. The effect of immersion is caused by illusory stimuli in the virtual system. In addition to individual coaching, group coaching can also be carried out in virtual worlds.

Avatar-based coaching is offered, for example, in the *CAI* (Cyber Anthropometric Intelligence) *system* by the Karlsruhe Institute for Coaching. The 'coached' moves as an avatar in a virtual world and is accompanied by an avatar as a coach. This virtual world with its natural scenery invites the coached to relax. Communication takes place via text or text messages and/or telephone systems.

Another format is *SimCoach*. It is a low-threshold offer to the US military to give soldiers initial orientation after a deployment and offers help with post-traumatic stress syndrome. The affected person can anonymously get in touch with an avatar who offers concrete help.

In the BMBF research focus *InterEmotio,* on the other hand, the *EmpaT* project was developed. This is an interactive 3D training environment for job interviews. The aim is to assess and improve social and emotional skills in an interactive dialogue, a simulated job interview, using virtual avatars.

An interactive, mobile assistance system is *EmmA* (emotional mobile avatar), which provides individual counselling in the event of mental stress. In addition, the system can be used for risk assessment at the workplace as well as company reintegration after a mental illness. EmmA is a coaching assistant that performs a multimodal real-time sensor analysis. It records and interprets physiological and social signals with the help of sensors in the smartphone of the respective user. Based on this, a socio-emotional behavioural model is developed and coupled to the virtual avatar, which offers context-dependent help in difficult situations.

There is also software that can recognize emotions via a camera and adaptively respond to clients. Many other examples can be named.

Outlook: Future and Development of Digital Psychology

It is no longer a question of *whether,* but *how* we deal with the advancing digitaliza-tion and how psychologists will position themselves here. There will be individual, economic and social improvements, but also "digital gaps" (Berufsverband Deutscher Psychologinnen und Psychologen 2018). Where innovations and im-provements arise in the digital space, it is also important to look at things critically. This includes accompanying phenomena such as hate speech and public outcries, deep fake, trolls, viruses, worms, data espionage and the darknet. Human-driven actions are linked to specific goals, desires, needs and hopes. The digital age forces us to rethink all areas of our lives and requires a strong will to shape them.

At present, little is known about the interrelationships of human thought, feel-ing and behaviour in the digital space. Perhaps it is not so important how the digital world can be described, but rather how we shape it. What is certain, however, is that – based on a humanistic view of mankind – the individual also wants to de-velop and evolve freely in the digital space. Psychology can support such active shaping. Certainly, within the new psychological discipline – *digital psychology* – different approaches will stand side by side on an equal footing and provide an-swers to questions from different perspectives. This will once again increase the complexity of the subject of psychology. It will also (have to) open up to new cur-rents and integrate them into the considerations of psychology.

In order to establish the research field of digital psychology, there is a need for an overview of the digital methods and interventions already in use, of research publications and accreditations, of topics offered and of evaluations. There is also a need for quality assurance in the field of digital psychology. The thematic field of digital psychology should, on the one hand, provide content transfer. On the other hand, it should also support the shaping and deepening of a person's personality in

M. Metz, B. Spies, *Digital Psychology*, essentials, https://doi.org/10.1007/978-3-658-40339-3_4

relation to digitalization. This includes the possibility of forming an attitude and thus generating sustainable knowledge and ethical behaviour for a life with digitality and virtuality. Topics such as (social) inequality, which is reinforced by digitalization and digital media, must be named and dealt with.

Perhaps digitalization is the engine for a new **turn in psychology.** The digitally induced cultural and social change must be actively shaped by people, even if it requires a certain expenditure of resources.

> A consciously unconscious waiting and letting things happen, a culturally uncritical standing on the sidelines is just as inadvisable as a digital euphoria that takes no notice of previous scientific research, for we are in the midst of change.

The train of digitalization has started rolling with the creative power of psychologists, but has been neglected when it comes to driving. Now it is time to jump back on the bandwagon and to co-determine and redefine the direction and thematic fields of psychology. It is not only a search for the right measure, but also a search for shaping the digital space along our values.

Appendix A. What You Can Take Away in this *Essential*

- Digitalization has long arrived in psychology.
- Digital means and methods can support and accompany the integration and participation of people.
- Psychologists should actively participate and help shape the emerging field of digital psychology for the benefit of human beings.
- The possibilities and limits of digital psychology must be uncovered and implemented by psychologists through the classification and delimitation of development and research fields.
- The definition, delimitation and development of the field of digital psychology should be further discussed and developed.

© The Author(s), under exclusive license to Springer Fachmedien   33
Wiesbaden GmbH, part of Springer Nature 2023
M. Metz, B. Spies, *Digital Psychology*, essentials,
https://doi.org/10.1007/978-3-658-40339-3

References

Baacke, D. (1996). Medienkompetenz – Begrifflichkeit und sozialer Wandel. In: Rein, A. (Hrsg.): *Medienkompetenz als Schlüsselbegriff* (S.112–124). Bad Heilbrunn: Klinkhardt.

Bartle, Richard A. (2006). *Designing virtual worlds*. [Nachdr.]. Berkeley, CA: New Riders.

Bartmann, F.J & Blettner, M. (2012). *Telemedizinische Methoden in der Patientenversorgung. Anwendungsspektrum, Chancen, Risiken*. Köln: Deutscher Ärzteverlag.

Batinic, B. & Appel, M. (Hrsg.). (2008) *Medienpsychologie*. Heidelberg: Springer Verlag.

Berufsverband Deutscher Psychologinnen und Psychologen (2018). *Mensch und Gesellschaft im digitalen Wandel*. https://www.bdp-verband.de/binaries/content/assets/verband/bdp-berichte/bdp-bericht-2018.pdf. Accessed: 22. April 2020.

Birbaumer, N. & Matuz, T. (2013). Brain-computer-interfaces (BCI) zur Kommunikation und Umweltkontrolle. In: Achim Stephan; Sven Walter (Hrsg.). *Handbuch Kognitionswissenschaft* (S. 239–247). Stuttgart, Weimar: J. B. Metzler.

Boes, A.; Gül, K.; Kämpf, T.; Langes, B.; Lühr, T.; Mars, K.; Vogl, E. & Ziegler, A.(2018). *Sillicon Valley: Vorreiter im digitalen Umbruch. Folgen für Deutschland und Europa*. Forschungsreport. München.

Bundesministerium für Gesundheit (2020). *Digitale-Versorgung-Gesetz*. https://www.bundesgesundheitsministerium.de/digitale-versorgung-gesetz.html. Accessed: 9 August 2020.

Bundesministerium für Wirtschaft und Energie (2019). *Bundeshaushalt 2020*. https://www.bmwi.de/Redaktion/DE/Artikel/Ministerium/haushalt-2020.html. Accessed: 9 August 2020.

Christakis, N. A. & Fowler, J. H. (2011). *Die Macht sozialer Netzwerke. Wer uns wirklich beeinflusst und warum Glück ansteckend ist*. Frankfurt a.M.: Fischer.

Damasio, A. (2017). *Im Anfang war das Gefühl. Der biologische Ursprung menschlicher Kultur*. München: Siedler Verlag.

Deinet, U.; Reis, C.; Reutlinger, C. & Winkler, M. (2018). *Potentiale des Aneignungskonzeptes*. Weinheim und München: Beltz Juventa Verlag.

© The Author(s), under exclusive license to Springer Fachmedien Wiesbaden GmbH, part of Springer Nature 2023
M. Metz, B. Spies, *Digital Psychology*, essentials,
https://doi.org/10.1007/978-3-658-40339-3

Duden (2020): *Cyber*. https://www.duden.de/suchen/dudenonline/cyber.Accessed: 9. August 2020.

Floridi, V., (2015). *Digitale Unternehmen haben ontologische Macht*. In: philosophie magazin 06/2015. S. 68–73. Philosophiemagazinverlag. Berlin.

Gabriel, M. (2018). *Der Sinn des Denkens*. Berlin: Ullstein Buchverlag GmbH.

Görgen, B. & Wendt, B. (2015). *Nachhaltigkeit als Fortschritt denken. Grundrisse einer soziologisch fundierten Nachhaltigkeitsforschung*. Soziologie und Nachhaltigkeit (SuN) – Beiträge zur sozial- ökologischen Transformationsforschung. Ausgabe 1/2015.1–21.

Hertzberg, J. (2013). Kognitive Robotik. In: A. Stephan & S. Walter (Hrsg.). *Handbuch Kognitionswissenschaft* (S. 47–51). Stuttgart, Weimar: J. B. Metzler.

Honneth, A. (2015). *Hegel und die Anerkennung*. In: philosophie magazin 05/2015, S. 78–81. Philosophiemagazinverlag. Berlin.

Huth, J. (2013). Informatik. In: A. Stephan & S. Walter (Hrsg.). *Handbuch Kognitionswissenschaft* (S. 42–43). Stuttgart, Weimar: J. B. Metzler.

Frauenhofer Institut (2018): *Spinnenphobie per Augmented Reality therapieren*. https://www.fraunhofer.de/de/presse/presseinformationen/2018/oktober/spinnenphobie-per-augmented-reality-therapieren.html. Accessed: 7. Mai 2020.

Kuhl, J.; Scheffer, D.; Mikoleit, B. & Strehau, A. (2010). *Persönlichkeit und Motivation im Unternehmen. Anwendungen der PSI-Theorie in Personalauswahl und -entwicklung*. 1. Auflage 2010 W. Stuttgart: Kohlhammer.

Löw, M. (2001). *Raumsoziologie*. Frankfurt am Main: Suhrkamp.

Pauen, M. & Welzer, H. (2015). *Autonomie. Eine Verteidigung*. Frankfurt am Main: S. Fischer.

Rao, A. & Georgeff, M. (1991). Modeling rational agents within a BDI-Architectur. In: *Proceeding of the 2nd International Conference on Principles of Knowledge Representation and Reasoning*. San Fransisco, 473–484.

Reutlingen, C. & Deinet, U. (2019). *Sozialraumarbeit und digital werdende Lebenswelten Jugendlicher. Nur hinterher kommen zu wollen, ist nicht genug aus!* Sozialmagazin, die Zeitschrift für soziale Arbeit (44 Jg.) Weinheim und München: Beltz Juventa. 6–12.

Rohde, M. (2013). Evolutionäre Robotik, organic computing und künstliches Leben. In: A. Stephan; & S. Walter (Hrsg.). *Handbuch Kognitionswissenschaft* (S. 180–183). Stuttgart, Weimar: J. B. Metzler.

Schmidt, U. (2013). Künstliche-Intelligenz-Forschung. In: A. Stephan; & S. Walter (Hrsg.). *Handbuch Kognitionswissenschaft* (S. 44–47). Stuttgart, Weimar: J. B. Metzler.

Stifterverband (2020). *Bildung. Wissenschaft. Innovation. Hochschul-Bildung-Report 2020. Für morgen befähigen*. Jahresbericht 2019. https://www.stifterverband.org/medien/hochschul-bildungs-report-2020-bericht-2019. Accessed: 2. Mai 2020.

Sühlmann-Faul, F., (2019). *Digitalisierung & Nachhaltigkeit: Risiken, Chancen und notwendige Schritte*. https://www.informatik-aktuell.de/management-und-recht/digitalisierung/risiken-und-chancen-der-digitalisierung.html. Accessed: 29. Juni 2020.

Sullivan, J. & Tyler, S. (1991). *Intelligent User Interfaces*. New York.

TKK (2020): *VR-Therapie bei Angststörungen*. https://wirtechniker.tk/2020/01/29/invirto-digitale-vr-therapie-bei-angststoerungen/. Accessed: 29. Juni 2020.

Treml, Alfred K. (2004). *Evolutionäre Pädagogik. Eine Einführung*. Stuttgart: Kohlhammer GmbH.

Trepte, S. & Reinecke, L. (2013). *Medienpsychologie*. Stuttgart: Kohlhammer.

Vdek (2019): *vdek-Zukunftsforum 2019. Schafft die Digitalisierung die Psychotherapeuten ab?*https://www.vdek.com/presse/pressemitteilungen/2019/zukunftsforum-2019-digitalisierung-psychotherapie.html. Accessed: 29. Juni 2020.

Verhaeghe, P. (2013). *Und ich? Identität in einer durchökonomisierten Gesellschaft.* München: Kunstmann.

Wachsmuth, I (2013). Mensch-Maschine-Interaktion. In: A. Stephan & S. Walter (Hrsg.). *Handbuch Kognitionswissenschaften* (S. 361–364). Stuttgart Weimar: J.B. Metzler.

WBGU – Wissenschaftlicher Beirat der Bundesregierung Globale Umweltveränderung (2011). *Factsheet. Globale Trends. Nr. 3/2011.* https://www.wbgu.de/fileadmin/user_upload/wbgu/publikationen/factsheets/fs3_2011/wbgu_fs3_2011.pdf. Accessed: 22 Januar 2020.

WBGU – Wissenschaftlicher Beirat der Bundesregierung Globale Umweltveränderung (2018). *Digitalisierung: worüber wir reden müssen.* https://www.wbgu.de/de/publikationen/publikation/digitalisierung-worueber-wir-jetzt-reden-muessen. Accessed: 04. Januar 2020.

WBGU – wissenschaftlicher Beirat der Bundesregierung Globale Umweltveränderungen (2019a). *Unsere gemeinsame digitale Zukunft. Zusammenfassung.* Berlin: WBGU.

WBGU – Wissenschaftlicher Beirat der Bundesregierung Globale Umweltveränderungen (2019b): *Unsere gemeinsame digitale Zukunft. Zusammenfassung.* https://www.wbgu.de/fileadmin/user_upload/wbgu/publikationen/hauptgutachten/hg2019/pdf/WBGU_HGD2019_Z.pdf. Accessed: 04. Januar 2020.

Ziemann, A. (2011): *Medienkultur und Gesellschaftsstruktur.* Soziologische Analysen. Wiesbaden: VS Verlag.